My Grandpa Nate

WRITTEN BY
Dr. Kelli M. Felder
ILLUSTRATED BY **Leena Shariq**

© Copyright 2025, My PreciousApple Publishing LLC

All rights reserved.

No part of this book may be used or reproduced mechanically, including photocopying, recording, taping, or any information storage retrieval system, without the publisher's written permission, except for brief quotations embodied in critical articles and reviews.

ISBN: 978-1-7350450-7-8

To my beloved grandfather,

Nathaniel Hall,

You were my teacher, my friend, and my biggest supporter. Your wisdom shaped my mind, your kindness nurtured my heart, and your unwavering belief in me gave me the courage to chase my dreams. This book is a tribute to the love, lessons, and legacy you left behind.

Forever grateful, forever inspired.

With love,
Your Granddaughter Kelli

My Grandpa's name is Nathaniel Hall, and he is my best friend. He is tall, wears glasses, is a sharp dresser, and is very smart. He's about 6'2", has really nice American suits, and the finest African clothes most people have ever seen. He reads all the time and is really into technology. He has all the finest and latest gadgets in his house and car. My Grandpa loves me, and he tells me so all the time.

He loves traveling to different parts of Africa, attending concerts, festivals, lectures, and eating soul food and pound cake. When he does his favorite things, he usually includes me. Grandpa also likes watching Law & Order and Wheel of Fortune.

He never, and I mean never, misses the Michigan Lottery at 7:30 pm. Whatever he is doing, Grandpa cuts it short, so he is home or somewhere near a television where he can watch the lottery.

Grandpa served in World War II. My great-grandmother, Grandpa's mother, proudly had his army photograph on the wall in her living room. He never spoke to me about his time in the war, but I know he was proud that he served our country.

My Grandpa also used to own a fleet of cabs and would drive me to school in his favorite cab, City Cab #604. Grandpa was not a morning person, but he would get out of his bed early every school day, sometimes in rainy, snowy, and very hot weather, and drive to my house to take me to school because I did not want to ride the school bus. My momma would tell Grandpa he was spoiling me, but he did not care. He still came every school day.

Grandpa would hold his hand on the car's horn to let the neighborhood and me know he was outside. Some neighbors would fuss about his horn waking them up, so I tried hard to be out the door before he turned the corner of my street. All my friends in the neighborhood and at school thought I was cool because I was coming to school in a cab and not a regular car or the school bus. Somedays, I would sit in the back of the cab, and we would talk through the plexiglass window. I sometimes put pennies in the money slot to act like a paying customer, and we would both laugh about that.

One time, when we had show-and-tell at my school, Grandpa came and spoke to my class about his visit to Egypt. He brought in some of the artwork, statues, and pictures he had taken. After that, my friends and I started to call our friend group the Egypt Group.

My grandpa also dressed up as Santa Claus at my school, but I got a little jealous that all the school kids were talking to him, so I told everyone that he wasn't the real Santa but my Grandpa. He didn't get mad; he just laughed and said, "Oh, Kelli."

Outside of school, on the weekends, and during the summer, it was our time to have more fun. Grandpa had a lot of friends, but he always made time for me and him. He would call me and say, "Get ready." Most of the time, I didn't know where we were going, but I knew it would be fun.

When we got together, Grandpa would tell me to squeeze him. He'd say, "Squeeze me, squeeze me," and that meant to give him a tight, tight hug. I would squeeze him so hard that I would feel my whole body shake. I would love to hear him call my name "Kel-Lee," or he'd call me "Black girl."

Grandpa used "Black girl" as a term of love and endearment. He loved Black people and culture and saw good in everything related to them.

Grandpa believed in me and supported everything I did. If I said I wanted to paint, he would sit still and let me paint him. If I wanted to play my clarinet, then Grandpa would turn down his hearing aids and let me practice for hours. He came to my dance recitals, school plays, and concerts. Grandpa was more to me than my mom's father. He was my best friend.

He would often take me to Belle Isle, the Hart Plaza weekly festivals in the summer, Big Boys, IHOP, and the neighborhood mom-and-pop restaurants he would frequently eat at. At the breakfast restaurants, he always got coffee with a lot of cream and sugar, sunny-side-up eggs that he'd put way too much salt on (yuck), sausage, and wheat toast. He let me order whatever I wanted and as much as I wanted.

I remember how the waitresses at the mom-and-pop restaurants would look on in amazement at all the Silver Dollar pancakes I could eat. Outside of eating, Grandpa also took me to many lectures to hear from historians like Dr. John Henrik Clark, Dr. Ben, and others who talked about African Americans, African diaspora, and Black history.

Grandpa loved music and talk radio. He would either play music or talk radio most of the time we rode in his car. He would wave his hand in the air when listening to some of his favorite songs by Aretha Franklin, Motown artists, and Billie Holiday. He played his favorite songs so much that I could sing along with the singers. I even started to like the talk radio shows. His favorite talk radio host was a lady named Martha Jean the Queen. She would talk and argue with people who called into her show about different things happening in Detroit and around the world.

On our trips to Belle Isle, Grandpa would take me and sometimes my friends to the Giant Slide and the playscape. We also went to Belle Isle and just sat by the water and talked. Sometimes, Grandpa would read the newspaper or a book, and I would play with other kids on the island, chase the seagulls, or get my book out and read.

At Hart Plaza, we would listen to music, eat, shop, and meet new and old friends. Grandpa would buy me dolls, clothes, and anything else I asked for. People liked my Grandpa and would always talk to him. We would stay at Hart Plaza all day and into the night. There was a fountain of water that Grandpa would let me run through on really hot days, and sometimes, he would only allow me to get my feet wet.

Most people who really knew my Grandpa knew he loved to read and had the biggest and best home library collection many people had ever seen. He encouraged me to read and often bought me books we would discuss. He was always teaching me something, and I thought we were just talking and having fun for a long time.

Grandpa was a big sports fan and loved boxing. His love of sports rubbed off on me, and we often watched sports together. He once bought us tickets to go and see the world heavyweight boxing champion compete for his title.

At the arena, I asked Grandpa if we could get popcorn before the fight started, and before we got settled back in our seats or before I could stick my hand in the popcorn box, the match was over. The champion had defended his title and knocked his competitor out in less than two minutes into the first round. Grandpa spent hundreds of dollars on the tickets, and the fight was not five minutes long. Grandpa didn't get mad; he just said, "Grab your popcorn and let's go."

When my Grandpa was younger, he fell down a flight of stairs and lost his hearing in his left ear. He wore hearing aids since I was born and spoke much louder than most people. Grandpa never allowed his hearing to stop him from doing anything he wanted to do. He told me some people tried to make things hard for him because he was a Black man, had a hearing disability, and spoke his mind.

He taught me that I was special, to believe in myself, to respectfully speak my mind, to face whatever challenges I have head-on, and to keep moving forward.

So, when Grandpa got sick, that was my first real challenge. I knew our lives were changing, and accepting this change was an adjustment for us both.

Grandpa started losing a lot of weight and then was unable to walk or drive. He had to move into our home with my mom, sister, and I. My dad had passed away many years ago. Grandpa no longer drove me to school, and our weekend outings ended. He did not like being in the house, but he was not strong enough to go outside. I realized it was now my turn to show up for him like he showed up for me. I could not take him out to have fun, so I had to bring the fun inside to him.

We still watched Law & Order, Wheel of Fortune, and the Michigan Lottery; we just didn't leave the house together for anything other than Grandpa's doctor appointments. I made sure we connected like we always did, just inside the house.

We would still talk about our family, the news, what happened at my school, books he wanted me to read, and a bunch of other stuff. We played checkers and cards, solved crossword puzzles, and searched the internet.

Grandpa would wait for me to get home from school every day, and I would be ready to share my best and funniest stories that I knew would make him laugh and smile. I tried hard to make him as happy as he made me, and it worked. His face would light up whenever I walked into his bedroom.

During this time at home with Grandpa, I learned that love is not about going to a bunch of places or spending a bunch of money but about being there for people who have always been there for you when they need you the most. Overall, I'm so grateful I can still spend time with Grandpa and tell and show him I love him, just like he's always told and shown me.

"Okay, so what do you think, Ms. Wilson? I completed the writing assignment and answered all the points in the rubrics. Is my essay good?" asked Kelli.

"Yes, Kelli, your essay is more than good; it's great! You were to write about someone who has shown you love, and you did that. There is no question that your granddad loves you, and you love him too, from the experiences you wrote about. I want you to type your paper and print two copies. One for the program and the other for you to present to your grandfather. He sounds like such a remarkable man, and I am sure he will appreciate hearing what you wrote about him during our school's Appreciation Night", replied Ms. Wilson.

Ms. Wilson gave Kelli an invitation addressed to Mr. Nathaniel Hall for her grandfather to attend the school's Appreciation Night Ceremony. Even though Kelli understood he would have to watch it on Zoom, she knew her Grandpa would be more than happy to be recognized in the program.

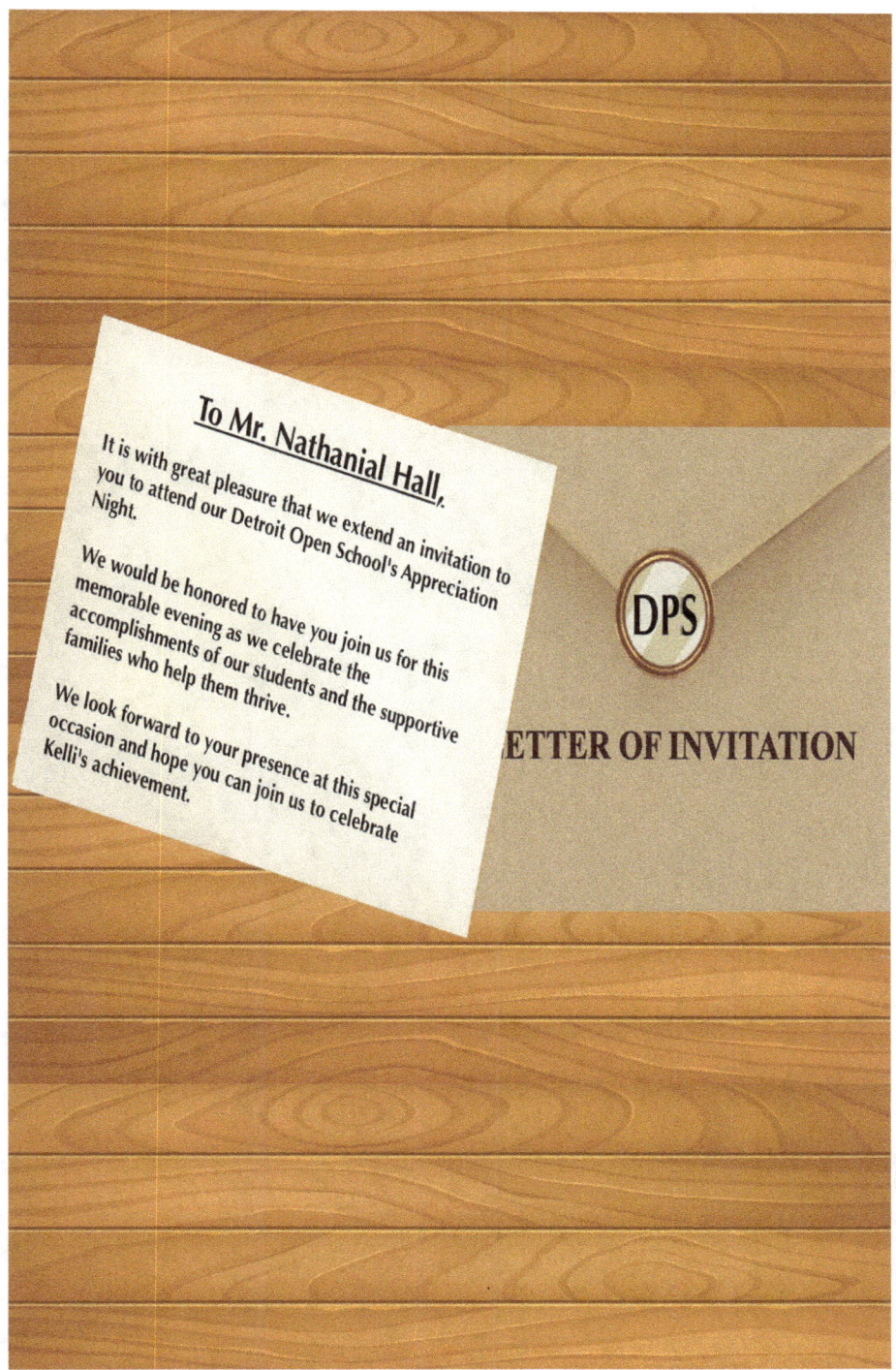

To Mr. Nathanial Hall,

It is with great pleasure that we extend an invitation to you to attend our Detroit Open School's Appreciation Night.

We would be honored to have you join us for this memorable evening as we celebrate the accomplishments of our students and the supportive families who help them thrive.

We look forward to your presence at this special occasion and hope you can join us to celebrate Kelli's achievement.

LETTER OF INVITATION

Questions

1. There are seven continents in the world. What continent did Grandpa travel to?

2. Sacrifice means to give up something you value to help others. Grandpa sacrificed his time and comfort for Kelli each school day by doing what?

3. How did things change for Grandpa and Kelli once Grandpa became sick?

4. Why did Kelli write the essay about her Grandpa?

5. At the conclusion of the book, Kelli discovers that real love is not about spending money or going places. What did she learn about the true meaning of love?

www.ingramcontent.com/pod-product-compliance
Lightning Source LLC
Chambersburg PA
CBHW072138070526
44585CB00016B/1739